Billy's Brain
And how it works differently

Written by Tammie Lee
Illustrated by Cassie Ward

For Tyler. Boisterous, brilliant and beautiful.

First published in 2022 by Tamcan Pty Ltd
Text Copyright © Tamcan Pty Ltd 2022
Illustrations Copyright © Cass e Ward 2022

All rights reserved in accordance with the Australian Copyright Act 1968. No part of this book may be reproduced in any form, by any means (electronic or mechanical), without prior written consent from the copyright owners.

National Library of Australia Cataloguing-in-Publication entry:

Lee, Tammie, 2022
Billy's Brain and how it works differently
ISBN: 978-0-6454582-0-6

Tamcan Pty Ltd acknowledges Australia's First Nations Peoples – the First Australians – as the Traditional Owners and Custodians of the land this book was written on, and gives respect to the Elders, past, present and emerging.

Hi, I'm Billy, and this is my brain.

My brain tells my body what to do.

"Time for a drink, you're thirsty!"

It helps me decide the things that I like...

...and the things that I don't like.

"I'm not sure about this; it looks different."

"This is so much fun!"

My brain lets me know when I am feeling happy...

...and when I'm feeling sad.

It even lets me know when I'm angry.

"Why won't our parents let us do what we want?"

My brain also lets me know when things are a bit too much for me...

"It's too noisy!"

"Much better with headphones!"

...so that it can keep me safe.

My brain has great ideas.

"I am good at lots of things!"

"We are too tired."

Sometimes, my brain can't think clearly...

...and it forgets to tell me what to do.

When my brain forgets, it makes me feel confused or angry, and I don't know what is going on.

But if we take a break...

Or do the things that make us feel good...

"This helps me to feel calm, you should try it too!"

Then we can feel happy again!

"Lets go and play!"

Everyone has a brain.

But my brain works differently to most people.

"Let us tell you!"

"I'm not sure what you mean"

My brain sees the world differently.

"Mmm, our favourite food, we know this is safe!"

My brain likes it when things are familiar.

It likes special things that sometimes people don't understand.

"Why doesn't everyone like this as much as me?"

My brain needs things to make sense.

"Do you like my new dress?"

"No."

And it is REALLY good at helping me tell the truth.

I need people to understand my brain...

"We like you just as you are!"

...and give me support.

Different ways to communicate.
Talk about feelings.
Learn about my needs.
Use helpful pictures.
Respect my differences.

So that it can keep giving me good ideas!

I don't mind that my brain works differently...

because without it...

I wouldn't be me!

For tips on reading this book to your child, including prompts for conversation starters, follow the link in the QR code below: